Kids in the Kitchen!

Let's Get Cooking

Here are some important rules for safe and successful cooking.

Keep Things Clean

- Always wash your hands. Do this before cooking, and after handling food.
- Wear an apron to keep your clothes clean. If you have long hair, tie it back.

Get Things Ready

- Read the recipe before you start cooking.
- Collect all the things you need before you begin.
- Weigh or measure out the things you will be using.
- Switch the oven on before you need to use it so it gets hot enough. It may take 10 or 15 minutes.
- When things are cooking in the oven, don't keep opening the door. Look through the window instead.

Ovens

- This sign tells you that you need to turn on the oven or grill.
- Electric oven temperatures are in centigrade, eg $200^{\circ}C$, or fahrenheit, eg $450^{\circ}F$. If your oven is fan-assisted, you may need to reduce cooking times. Look at the handbook.
- Gas oven temperature controls use gas marks, eg gas mark 4.

Keep Things Safe

- Knives are very sharp! Use them very carefully with help from a grown-up.

- If you need to use anything electrical, get a grown-up to help. Never touch anything electrical with wet hands.

- Cooked food and ovens can be very hot. Always wear oven gloves when taking food from the oven or grill.

- Turn saucepan handles to the side so you do not knock them and spill hot food.

Keep Things Tidy

- Always tidy up when you've finished cooking. Do the washing up, or load the dishwasher, and put things back where they came from.

Equipment

- Here are some of the things you will need:

kitchen scales	sieve	cooling rack
measuring spoons	pastry brush	peeler
measuring jug	wooden spoon	vegetable brush
baking trays	chopping board	grater
mixing bowl	saucepans and lids	whisk

Measuring

- Use kitchen scales to measure dry ingredients.

- Use measuring spoons to measure spoonfuls. All spoon measures are level, not heaped. Skim off any extra using a knife.

- Use a measuring jug to measure liquids.

Get Help

- Kitchens can be dangerous places! Always cook with a grown-up to help you, and take extra care when you see this sign.

And last of all ... have fun!

7

Smoothies and Shakes

Fruit smoothies and shakes taste great — and they are very quick and easy to make.

Banana and Apple Smoothie

To make 2 smoothies you need:

- 1 large banana
- 150g pot plain yogurt
- 2 teaspoons honey
- 60ml apple juice
- 1 lemon

IDEA! Use fruit yogurt instead of plain.

IDEA! If the smoothie is too thick, stir in a little more apple juice.

1.

Peel the banana and cut it into thick slices.

2.

Put the banana, yogurt, honey and apple juice into a blender or food processor.

3.

Ask a grown-up to blend until smooth, then pour into tall glasses and put a straw in each.

4.

Cut two thin slices of lemon. Cut from the edge to the centre of each slice and sit on the rim of each glass.

Strawberry Shake

To make 2 shakes
you need:

- 125g strawberries
- 150ml milk

1.

Rinse the strawberries and cut
off the green tops.

2.

Put the strawberries and milk
into a blender and ask a
grown-up to blend until bubbly
and frothy.

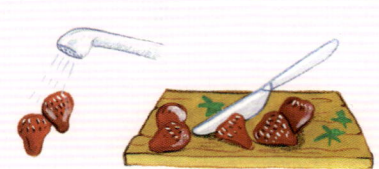

IDEA! Add a scoop of
vanilla ice cream or some
crushed ice for a cooling
summer shake.

IDEA! Float a strawberry half on top.

Try these smoothies, or make up your
own using the fruits you like best:

flesh of
1 peach   +   125g
raspberries   +   125ml
orange juice   =   Sunny
Smoothie

flesh of 1
ripe mango   +   200ml
cranberry juice   +   150ml pot
peach yogurt   =   Tropicana

Potato Bakes

Baked potatoes are easy to make – and you can have fun adding your favourite fillings!

Buttery Bakes

For each baked potato you need:

- 1 large baking potato
- 2 teaspoons butter

Preheat the oven to 200°C, 400°F or gas mark 6.

SERVE with a mixed or green salad.

1.

Wash the potato and scrub it, using a vegetable brush. Take out any 'eyes' or bad bits.

2.

Prick the potato 3 or 4 times on each side with a fork. Put it on a baking tray.

3.

Bake in the oven for at least 1 hour. Ask a grown-up to test if the potato is cooked.

4.

Wearing oven gloves, cut a cross in the top of the potato. Push the base to open up the potato, and add butter.

You can add all sorts of toppings to your baked potato, like these:

Beany Bake

Empty a small tin of baked beans into a pan. Heat until warm.

Tuna-Sweetcorn Bake

Drain a small tin of tuna and a small tin of sweetcorn. Break up the tuna with a fork and mix with the sweetcorn. Add a little mayonnaise.

Cheesy Bake

Grate 30-40g Cheddar cheese coarsely. Add some chopped chives.

Cheddar-Cottage Bake

Grate 20g Cheddar cheese and mix with 30g cottage cheese. Top with chopped herbs.

Chilli Bake

Make the Bolognese sauce recipe on page 14 and mix 3 tablespoons with a small tin of red kidney beans (drained) and a pinch of chilli powder.

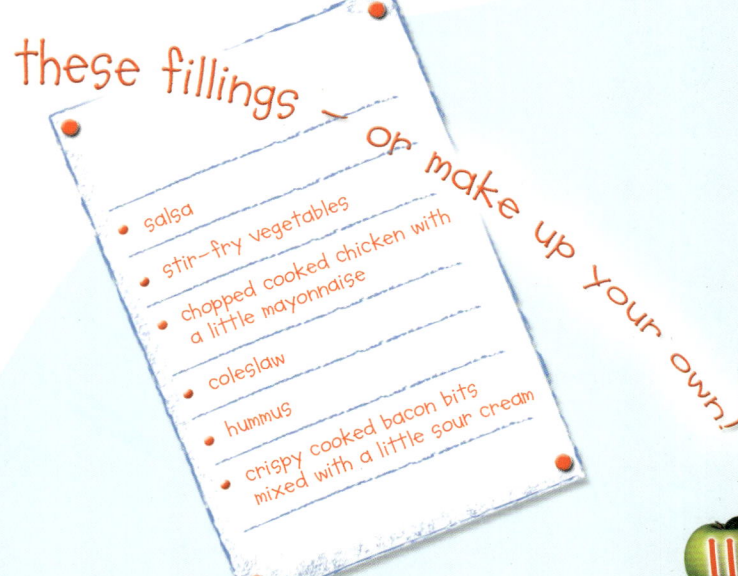

Try these fillings – or make up your own!

- salsa
- stir-fry vegetables
- chopped cooked chicken with a little mayonnaise
- coleslaw
- hummus
- crispy cooked bacon bits mixed with a little sour cream

Easy-Cheesy Burgers

The very best burgers are ones you make yourself at home!

Easy-Cheesy Burgers

To make 4 you need:

- 500g minced beef
- 1 small onion
- salt and pepper
- 1 egg
- 4 cheese slices
- lettuce
- 4 burger buns
- tomato relish or ketchup

 Turn on the grill.

1.

Chop the onion into very small pieces.

2.

Put the minced beef and onion into a bowl. Add some salt and pepper.

3.

Beat the egg and add to the meat.

4.
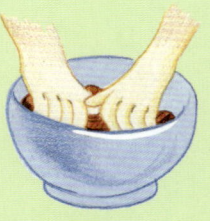
With VERY clean hands, press and squeeze the mixture until it sticks together.

5.

Divide into 4 pieces and roll into balls. Press flat to make burger shapes. Put on the rack of a grill pan.

6.

Cook under the grill for 5-8 minutes or until brown. Turn over and cook for another 5 minutes.

7.

Put a cheese slice on each burger and grill until the cheese melts.

8.

Cut the burger buns in half. Shred some lettuce and put it on the bottom half of the bun. Add the burger, some tomato relish or ketchup, and the top half of the bun.

Why not try some quick and easy Veggie Burgers?

1. Buy a pack of 4 vegetable or mycoprotein burgers. Cook them following the instructions on the packet.

2. Warm 4 wholemeal pitta breads under the grill. Cut along one side to open.

3. Fill with shredded lettuce, your favourite sauce or relish, some grated vegetarian cheese – and your burgers.

IDEA! Add some extras to make your burger super-special.
· mayonnaise · mild mustard · slices of tomato
· barbecue sauce · sweetcorn relish · crispy grilled bacon

IDEA! Use chicken or turkey mince instead of beef.

Perfect Pasta

Pasta tastes good with all kinds of sauces.
It's great energy food, so eat lots of it!

Spaghetti Bolognese

To make 4 helpings you need:

- 1 tablespoon olive oil
- 1 small onion
- 500g minced beef
- 400g tin chopped tomatoes
- 1 level teaspoon dried mixed herbs
- salt and black pepper
- 500g spaghetti
- 100g grated Cheddar cheese

IDEA! Use chicken, turkey or meat-free mince in place of beef.

IDEA! Sprinkle with a little grated Parmesan cheese instead of Cheddar.

1.

Chop the onion into small pieces. Heat the oil in a large pan and fry the onion for about 5 minutes, until it is soft.

2.

Put the beef into the pan. Stir and fry it for about 10-15 minutes, until it is brown and crumbly.

3.

Add the tomatoes, herbs, salt and pepper. Stir, put on a lid and simmer for 20 minutes.

4.

Heat some water and a pinch of salt in a big pan. When it boils, add the spaghetti and push down into the water. Boil for the number of minutes it says on the pack.

14

5.

Tip the cooked spaghetti into a colander over the sink to drain off the water.

6.

Put some spaghetti in a dish or on a plate and add the meat sauce. Sprinkle with grated cheese.

To make meat-free Penne Pasta:

1. Cook **500g penne pasta** following the directions on the pack.

2. Chop **1 clove garlic** finely. Heat **1 tablespoon oil** in a pan and fry the garlic for about 2 minutes.

3. Add **400g tin chopped tomatoes**, **1 teaspoon dried basil** (or a handful of fresh basil leaves), **a pinch of sugar** and **salt** and **pepper**.

4. Cook the sauce for 5 minutes, stir into the drained pasta and serve with fresh **basil leaves** if you have some.

IDEA! Pasta comes in all shapes, sizes - and colours! Use the kind you like best and cook it as on the pack.

IDEA! Add some **black olives** at step 3 if you like them.

Sweet Treats

Make this special treat by layering lots of yummy things in a tall glass.

Knickerbocker Glory

For each one you need:

- half a small carton whipping cream
- 1 pear
- 1 peach
- 6 strawberries
- 2 scoops chocolate ice cream
- 1 scoop strawberry ice cream
- 1 ice cream wafer
- cherries (fresh or glacé)
- 1 tube red dessert sauce

1.

Put the cream into a mixing bowl. Using a metal whisk, whip until it is thick and stiff.

2.

Wash the fruit.

3.

Peel the pear and cut off the stalk and base. Cut into 4 and take out the core. Cut into thin slices or pieces.

4.

Cut the peach in half and take out the stone. Cut into thin slices or pieces.

5.

Cut the green tops off the strawberries. Cut into thin slices.

6.

Mix the pear, peach and strawberry pieces. Put 1 tablespoon of the fruit mixture into the glass.

7.

Add 1 tablespoon cream and more fruit, then 2 scoops chocolate ice cream. Add more fruit and cream to fill the glass.

8.

Put the strawberry ice cream on top. Add a wafer and two cherries, then drizzle with red dessert sauce.

IDEA!
Add layers of jelly if you like. Choose your favourite, and make it up as on the pack. When it is set, chop it roughly and add between layers of fruit and cream.

Have fun making different kinds of sweet treats.
Try these – or make up your own.

chocolate flake

toffee ice cream

whipped cream

chopped bananas

toffee ice cream

chopped bananas

chopped nuts

whipped cream

toffee ice cream

chopped bananas

dessert biscuit

tiny chocolate buttons

whipped cream

raspberries

vanilla ice cream

raspberries

whipped cream

vanilla ice cream

raspberries

17

Sweetie Cookies

Crispy-coated chocolate sweets make these cookies extra-special!

Sweetie Cookies

To make about 15 you need:

- a little vegetable oil
- 200g plain flour
- 1 teaspoon bicarbonate of soda
- 125g soft brown sugar
- 125g butter
- 1 egg
- 150g crispy-coated chocolate sweets

 Preheat the oven to 180°C, 350°F or gas mark 4.

1.

Use a pastry brush and a little oil to grease 2 baking sheets.

2.

Use a sieve to sift the flour and bicarbonate of soda into a mixing bowl. Stir in the brown sugar.

3.

Cut the butter into tiny cubes and add to the bowl.

4.

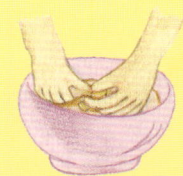

With VERY clean hands, use your fingertips and thumbs to rub the butter cubes into the flour. Do this gently! The mixture should look like breadcrumbs.

5.

Beat the egg with a fork. Pour into the bowl and mix in.

6.

Stir in the sweets.

7.

Drop spoonfuls of mixture onto the baking sheets. Leave space between them. Make sure some sweets are sticking out.

8.

Bake for about 10 to 12 minutes until the cookies are light brown. Wearing oven gloves, take out of the oven to cool.

You can use this recipe to make lots of different kinds of cookies.

 To make Jelly Cookies, add 150g jelly beans in place of the sweets.

 For Chunky Chocolate Cookies, use 150g chocolate in place of the sweets. Cut into little pieces before adding to the mixture.

 For Nutty Cookies, use 100g chopped hazelnuts in place of the sweets.

 For Fruity Cookies, use 100g raisins or sultanas in place of the sweets.

Yummy Cup Cakes

Cup cakes are easy to make – and lots of fun to ice and decorate!

Cup Cakes

To make about 20 you need:

- 125g self-raising flour
- 125g soft margarine (or butter)
- 125g caster sugar
- 2 eggs
- 1 teaspoon vanilla extract or essence

 Preheat the oven to 180°C, 350°F or gas mark 4.

1.

Put the butter and sugar into a mixing bowl. Use a wooden spoon to cream the mixture until it is smooth and fluffy.

2.

Beat in the eggs and vanilla extract, then stir in the flour. Mix until smooth.

3.

Put paper bun cases on a baking tray. Put a heaped teaspoon of mixture into each case so they are about half full.

4.

Put in the oven for about 15 minutes, until golden. If they are not ready, cook for another 2 or 3 minutes. Wearing oven gloves, put on a wire rack to cool.

To make the icing you need:

- 250g icing sugar
- 1-2 tablespoons water

You also need some cake decorations.

1. Sieve the icing sugar into a bowl.

2.  Add the water drop by drop and stir hard until it is all mixed in. The icing should be glossy and thick.

3. Cut any little lumps off the cakes so the tops are flat.

4. Use a spoon to put a little icing on each cake, then put a decoration on top.

IDEA! Colour the icing using food colouring. Add this drop by drop because a little bit makes a LOT of colour!

Add different toppings:

- mini fruit sweets
- chocolate chips or buttons
- silver or gold balls
- mini marshmallows
- mini fudge cubes

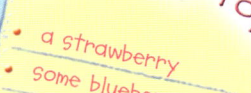

Try fruity toppings:

- a strawberry
- some blueberries
- a slice of banana
- a glacé cherry

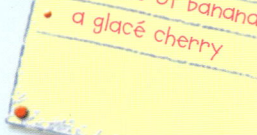

Idea! Make extra-special cup cakes:

Funny Faces

Add mini buttons or sweets for eyes and nose and use a tube of writing icing to add a smile.

Christmas

Top with white icing 'snow' and add mini holly decorations.

Parties

Use a tube of writing icing to write the first letters of your friends' names on top.

Halloween

Top with orange icing and a black sweet.